IMAGES
of England

STREATHAM

Streatham War Memorial, c. 1925.

IMAGES
of England

STREATHAM

Compiled by
John W. Brown
from the Johns Collection of Lambeth Archives

TEMPUS

First published 1999
Copyright © John W. Brown, 1999

Tempus Publishing Limited
The Mill, Brimscombe Port,
Stroud, Gloucestershire, GL5 2QG

ISBN 0 7524 1819 X

Typesetting and origination by
Tempus Publishing Limited
Printed in Great Britain by
Midway Clark Printing, Wiltshire

British Home and Hospital for Incurables, Crown Lane, *c.* 1912.

Contents

Acknowledgements

This book would not have been possible without the agreement of Lambeth Archives to make this wonderful collection of old photographs of Streatham available for reproduction. In this regard I am most grateful to the following members of staff for their valuable help and assistance: Jon Newman, Sue McKenzie, Gabrielle Bourn, Heather Warne, Graham Gower, Howard Falksohn, Tamar Baker, John Henderson and Maureen Manning.

I also extend my thanks to members of the Local History Group of the Streatham Society who have so freely shared the results of their researches with me over the years and in particular Brian Bloice, John Cresswell, Jill Dudman, Tony Fletcher, Betty Griffin, Brenda Hargreaves, Judy Harris, Keith Holdaway, Peter Jefferson-Smith, Bob Jenner, Kevin Kelly and Audrey Thomas.

My thanks also to Patrick Loobey, of 231 Mitcham Lane, Streatham, London SW16 6PY (telephone 020-8769 0072), who has an unrivalled collection of London postcards issued by Johns and is widely recognized as the leading expert on the company.

Finally I record my appreciation to my brother, Maurice, without whose continued assistance and valuable help this book would not have been possible.

John W. Brown

Immanuel church, Streatham High Road, c.1933.

Introduction

The name Streatham means the 'Hamlet on the Street' – Street Ham. This shows the origin of the town as a small cluster of houses along the ancient trackway which now forms part of the A23 London to Brighton road. For centuries the village was to remain a small and relatively insignificant community situated roughly halfway on the road between London and the Archbishop of Canterbury's palace at Croydon. The majority of villagers were poor and earned their living from working the land. It was while some of these agricultural labourers were toiling in a field at the top of Streatham Common that they made a discovery that was to play a major role in the future development of their village.

It was on a hot, dry day in the summer of 1659 that men weeding the field decided to quench their thirst from a nearby spring. Shortly after drinking they experienced the 'purging' effects of the water and thus discovered the benefits to be gained by drinking from what became known as Streatham Spa or Mineral Wells. News of the medicinal qualities of the water soon spread among the villagers who found that there was almost no end to the curative and recuperative powers of the water. After supping from the spring the local tailor found his sight vastly improved, while the locksmith feeling 'much consumed and very ill' partook of the water and within three days had passed four worms, one of which was 8ft 3in long!

By 1670 Streatham Spa had been developed into a major attraction and it was not uncommon for carriages to be seen stretching for a mile along Streatham High Road as Londoners flocked to the village to take the waters. Within a short space of time Streatham became a fashionable location and a number of wealthy merchants had established their country homes in the parish. Streatham's popularity as a select residential area continued long after the craze for medicinal waters had passed. By the mid-nineteenth century a number of fine mansions had been built by wealthy residents who were attracted to the parish by its rural charms and close proximity to London.

The opening of Streatham Hill railway station in 1856 brought the area within easy commuting distance of the capital and led to an influx of a large number of middle-class residents. Roads of large Victorian villas provided these new inhabitants with comfortable homes and firmly established the neighbourhood as a much sought-after locality in which to live.

Within the space of a generation the area changed almost beyond recognition. As the twentieth century dawned, Streatham had been transformed from a small country village into a bustling southern suburb of London. This change was captured on film by a local firm of photographers called R.C. Johns & Co., later to bcome Maycock & Johns. Based in Longley Road, Tooting, this company specialized in the production of picture postcards. Although the humble postcard is mainly associated today with the sending of holiday greetings to family and friends, it was for many years prior to the First World War the main means of popular communication. With numerous collections and deliveries each day it was possible to post a card in the morning to a local friend inviting them to dine that evening and to receive their acceptance in the afternoon post.

Mr Johns established his photographic business in 1911 and initially concentrated his output on the local neighbourhood, specializing in views of Tooting, Streatham and the surrounding area. Over the ensuing quarter of a century, the company was to build up a library of over 12,000 photographic views, chiefly of the southern and western suburbs of London.

In the early 1990s around 6,000 glass plates from which Johns printed their postcards were discovered in the attic of a house in Mitcham. This amazing discovery comprised almost half of the firm's negatives and included a number of views which had been taken by the company but appear never to have been issued as postcards. This collection was subsequently sold with appropriate views being acquired by the archives departments of the London Boroughs of Lambeth, Merton, Sutton and Wandsworth and the balance being bought by two private collectors.

The photographs contained in this book comprise most of the Streatham views purchased by Lambeth Archives. Although the Archives' holding does not contain all the Streatham photographs taken by Johns its strength lies in the large number of residential roads featured in their collection. Some of these were taken shortly after the last houses in the streets had been built as the roads remain muddy trackways, still to be surfaced. This is particularly so for those photographs of the streets on the Streatham Vale Estate taken in the mid-1920s.

To gather together over 200 old photographs of Streatham is no mean achievement in its own right. That they should all be taken by the same firm of photographers is an added bonus and makes this collection a unique record of the area in the opening decades of the twentieth century.

I hope this book will inspire residents of Streatham to discover more about the fascinating history of their suburb. In this regard they will find the staff at Lambeth Archives pleased to help them in their researches, whether they be interested in tracing the history of their home or family, or wish to find out more about a particular aspect of the development of the Borough. I encourage you to visit the Archives at the Minet Library, 52 Knatchbull Road, London SE5 9QY (tel: 020-7926 6076) to explore the wealth of local material which they have.

The Local History Group of the Streatham Society holds regular meetings at 8 p.m. on the first Monday of each month at Woodlawns, 16 Leigham Court Road, Streatham SW16. Illustrated talks on all aspects of Streatham's history are given, as well as workshop sessions, discussions and ephemera and collectable evenings at which members are encouraged to bring along items of interest. A warm welcome is extended to anyone interested in the history of the area or those wishing to discover more about Streatham's fascinating past.

I hope you will enjoy this collection of views of old Streatham through the lens of R.J. Johns & Co. and I would be delighted to hear from readers with their recollections of the area in bygone days.

John W. Brown
316 Green Lane,
Streatham,
London SW16 3AS.

Streatham High Road, *c.* 1912.

One
Streatham High Road

Streatham High Road, *c.* 1919. In the 1870s Streatham could still be described as a country town and the population of the parish was smaller than that of Haslemere in Surrey today. At that time Streatham High Road was a quiet thoroughfare and the fastest thing on the road was a cyclist pedalling down the hill! However, within the space of a generation all this was to change as the face of Streatham was altered from that of a small country town to a bustling London suburb. Fields that once grew crops suddenly sprouted roads of houses and the old inhabitants of the village quickly found themselves outnumbered by a huge wave of new residents. Nowhere was this change more evident than along Streatham High Road, where the old cottages and houses which once lined the street were swept away and replaced by large Victorian and Edwardian terraces of modern shops, as seen above.

Church Place and Western Terrace, Streatham High Road, *c.* 1919. The left-hand cottage in this row of ancient terraced properties was no. 5 Western Terrace, later known as no. 468 Streatham High Road. This was South Streatham's first sub-post office, which was opened by John and Elizabeth Abbiss in the late 1850s. Their daughter, Mary, served customers here for over sixty-five years until shortly before her death in January 1922 aged seventy-one.

Bank Parade, 426-450 Streatham High Road, *c.* 1912. The glass canopy which provided a covered walkway in front of Bank Parade can be seen between the trees on the right of this photograph. The architects for this building were Tooley & Son and it was erected in 1890 by William Marriage of Croydon. This building provided South Streatham with its first parade of modern shops. Note the young trees lining the High Road which have now grown into mighty horse chestnut trees.

Immanuel church, c. 1912. In 1854 a small chapel was erected here to cater for the spiritual needs of the residents of South Streatham. The rapidly increasing population of the area soon outgrew this building and the church seen here was erected in 1865. It was designed by the architect Benjamin Ferry, who incorporated the spire of the original church in his design which can be seen on the top of the tower.

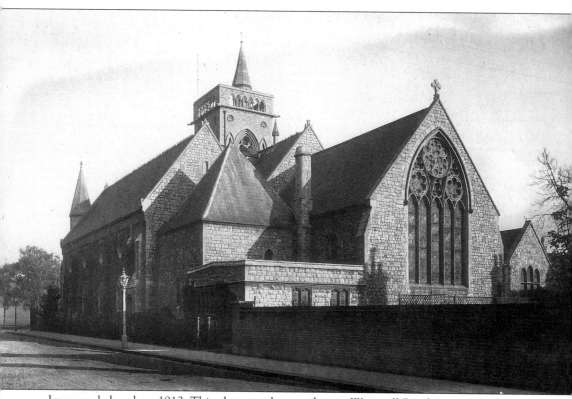

Immanuel church, *c.* 1912. This photograph was taken in Westwell Road Approach and shows the rear of the church with the subsequent additions to Ferry's original building. In 1987 the main part of the church was demolished and a new place of worship was built behind the tower which was left standing on the High Road. The remainder of the site was redeveloped with sheltered housing for the elderly which is called St John's House, after St John's College, Cambridge. This was the college attended by Revd Stenton Eardley, the first incumbent of Immanuel church, who served here from 1854 to 1883. The Revd Eardley was born near Chapel-en-le-Frith, Derbyshire, in 1821 and was ordained in 1846. When he came to Immanuel in 1854 the church served the small rural hamlet of South Streatham. This mainly comprised a cluster of houses around the northern end of Greyhound Lane and a few cottages at Lower Streatham, between Hermitage Lane and the River Graveney, beyond which lay open fields and pasture land as far as Thornton Heath. As the population of his parish grew, Revd Eardley was quick to adapt to the changing circumstances. Immanuel soon became known as one of the best-organized parishes in the country with day and Sunday schools, district visitors, church and temperance choirs, a band of hope, a medical club for the poor, a building society and a temperance society. For almost twenty-five years the Revd Eardley devoted much of his energy to fighting the evils of drink and he was well known nationally for his temperance work. In 1878 he raised £6,000 for the building of the Beehive Coffee Tavern and Assembly Rooms which were built next to the Pied Bull public house in Streatham High Road. This temperance hall provided a teetotal environment in which local residents and workmen could obtain wholesome meals and entertain themselves free from the temptation of drink. The building survives today and is now used as a solicitor's office. The Revd Eardley died in July 1883 and was buried at West Norwood Cemetery. As his cortège left Immanuel church a muffled peal of 5,040 changes were rung on the church bells. Twenty private carriages followed the coffin, with nearly 200 mourners on foot walking behind. Eardley Road in Streatham is named in his honour.

12

Greyhound Place, Streatham Common, *c.* 1925. The Bovril sign adorns one of the oldest buildings in the area. Known as The White House, this cottage dates back to the eighteenth century. The small building to the left was John Holt's Dining Rooms. John was a kindly man and from 1889 onwards unobtrusively did his best to alleviate the hardships the poor of the area had to endure. In 1901 he was presented with a gold watch by his friends in recognition of his generosity to others.

Bladon Terrace, Streatham High Road, *c.* 1928. This terrace stood between Barrow and Lewin Roads. Sir John Milton, Accountant-General of the Army, died at his home here on 29 November 1880. He joined the War Office in 1840 and in 1855 was appointed Purveyor-in-Chief of the Army in the Crimea for which service he was awarded the Crimean and Turkish War Medals. He served as Accountant-General from 1871 to 1878 and was knighted by Queen Victoria in January 1879.

Streatham Congregational church, Streatham High Road, c. 1930. Partly hidden behind the trees is the tower of the Congregational church which was built in 1901 to the designs of James Cubitt. Two major retailers were supporters of this church: Frank Bentall, who owned a department store in Kingston and lived in North Drive, Streatham Park, and Charles Derry, of Derry and Toms, who laid the foundation stone of the church on 16 May 1900. Mr Derry's daughter laid the foundation stone for the adjacent church hall on 24 October 1911, which was built on the site of the stables and conservatory of the large house called Heathfield that used to occupy this site.

Streatham High Road, c. 1912. The row of single-storey lock-up shops on the left of the upper photograph were known as Station Parade. James Boyle ran his shoe and boot-making business from no. 3 and in 1912 was responsible for apprehending three young French girls who stole a pair of shoes from his shop. Unbeknown to him at the time the young ladies were a group of notorious shoplifters who had been active in a number of leading West End stores including Selfridge's and Peter Robinson's. When police searched their lodgings in nearby Norbury they discovered a treasure trove of stolen goods. Such was the size of the hoard that two cabs were required to take the pile of pilfered items to the police station. These included 130 items of ladies' underwear, over 100 handkerchiefs, fourteen skirts, eleven coats, three shawls and two muffs. Station Parade was demolished in 1984 and the site is now occupied by a Safeway supermarket.

The Empire Picture Palace, Streatham High Road, *c.* 1912. This was one of the earliest cinemas to be built in Streatham and advertised itself as 'South London's largest and best ventilated hall'. As well as accommodating 1,200 film goers, it provided tea rooms, reading rooms and a billiard saloon with two tables. The cinema was built by Mr Chapman and was opened by Alderman Hewett in December 1910. In 1940 it was converted into a sporting club which was popular for its weekly dances. The hall was destroyed by a V1 bomb which scored a direct hit on the building on 17 June 1944.

The Bedford Park Hotel, Streatham High Road, *c.* 1925. In 1882 Arthur Kelday was given permission to build this pub on condition that the licence of the old Five Bells, which stood opposite Streatham Green, was surrendered. An early problem for the licensee here was the theft of empty beer bottles from the yard at the rear of the premises. These 'empties' would be taken by thirsty drinkers who would carry them up the High Road to the White Lion where they would claim the refund due. The cash would then be handed back to the barman as payment for a full bottle of beer.

The Triangle, 324-342 Streatham High Road, c. 1925. This parade of Victorian shops was designed by the architects Wheeler & Hollands and was built by Hill Brothers of Streatham in 1887. The Triangle originally consisted of seven large shops supplying retailers with 50ft of showroom space with access from both the High Road and Gleneagle Road. Prospective purchasers were offered the freehold interest in the shops as well as eight rooms of living accommodation above the premises.

The Dip, Streatham High Road, *c.* 1928. The stretch of Streatham High Road between St Leonard's church and Gleneagle Road was known as 'The Dip' because of the incline of the hill here. The view below shows the northern section of the road in around 1912. The signboard on the left hangs over Charles Humphreys' bookshop at no. 288 Streatham High Road and reads 'Brains Brains Ancient & Modern Bought Sold Exchanged'. Charles was a well-known second-hand bookseller who moved to Streatham in 1906. He used to cover the front of his premises with various improving texts and slogans to encourage trade such as 'This is the place where fools see nothing and wise men buy books cheap', 'If you kiss your wife half as much as you did when you were courting you would have a happy home', and the mysterious 'Pohs Paehc Lufrednow', which was 'Wonderful Cheap Shop' spelt backwards!

St Leonard's church, *c.* 1912. Streatham's parish church of St Leonard has stood at the junction of the High Road and Mitcham Lane for around 1,000 years and mention is made of a chapel at Streatham in the Domesday Survey compiled in 1086. On 3 January 1841 the spire was struck by lightning and despite the brave efforts of a villager called Sandy, who climbed the tower to try to extinguish the flames, it was destroyed in the blaze. A new spire was erected the following year at a cost of £650.

St Leonard's Church *c*. 1919. This view shows the interior of the chancel which was added to the church in 1863. This was designed by William Dyce, the pre-Raphaelite artist. He was churchwarden at St Leonard's from 1862 until his death in 1864 and is buried in the churchyard. Dyce was a member of the Royal Academy and his work can be seen in the Houses of Parliament, Buckingham Palace and at Osborn House on the Isle of Wight. In addition to his painting, he also designed the first florin, the modern-day equivalent of which is the 10p piece.

Interior of St Leonard's church, *c.* 1919. To the left of the arch is the magnificent Jacobean pulpit which stood in the church for over 300 years until it was lost in the fire which completely gutted the church in 1975. In 1649, Sir John Howland, Lord of the Manor of Streatham and Tooting Bec, left £10 in his will to cover the cost of a new pulpit for the church. To commemorate his bequest Sir John's arms were carved on the central panel of the pulpit.

St Leonard's churchyard *c.* 1912. Over the centuries thousands of local residents have been buried in the parish churchyard. Many of the graves have been reused over and over again and for most of those who were interred here no memorial or gravestone survives to mark their final resting place. One of the most intriguing burials here is that of 'Bet' Russell who died aged 104 on 14 April 1772 and who 'was always known under the guise or habit of a woman, and answered to the name of Elizabeth as registered in this Parish on November 21st 1669, but at death proved to be a man.'

Streatham High Road, *c.* 1912. The large building on the left was erected on part of the garden of the Rectory and was originally known as St Leonard's Terrace. This must have been confusing as the same name had earlier applied to a row of shops situated between Sunnyhill and Pinfold Roads. At no. 10 St Leonard's Terrace, Ellen Priddis manufactured mantles which were used on the gas lamps which at that time provided the main source of lighting in Streatham.

Streatham police station, *c.* 1912. Streatham's first police station was built in 1865 when only a handful of officers maintained law and order in the area. As the local population grew the need for a larger station became urgent and the old building was demolished in 1912 and replaced with the station seen here. To the right are the Thrale Almshouses which were built in 1832 by the family of Henry and Hester Thrale to provide accommodation for four poor women of the parish.

Streatham Library, Streatham High Road, *c.* 1926. The library was a gift to the people of Streatham by Sir Henry Tate of Park Hill (see p. 121). It was built in 1890, the architect being Sidney R.J. Smith, who did much work for Sir Henry and was the architect for the Tate Gallery in London. Opposite the Library is Pratt's Department Store which moved here from a small shop in Bedford Row, opposite Streatham Green, in 1867. This was the first shop to be built on this side of the High Road and continued to trade from this site until 1990. Originally the young shop assistants working at Pratt's lived in rooms above the shop, but these were later adapted for commercial use. The store was founded by George Pratt who came to Streatham in 1840 as a thirteen-year-old apprentice to William Reynolds, a local draper. George had a natural flare for business and quickly prospered. He became a large local landowner and developed the Bedford Park Estate.

The Astoria Cinema, Streatham High Road, *c.* 1933. Designed by E.A. Stone, the Astoria opened on 30 June 1930 and was one of the largest in the area, seating almost 3,000 people. The cinema had a huge stage, almost as large as that at Drury Lane Theatre. Here entertainments were performed between film screenings. As was common practice in the 1930s the Astoria also had a huge organ which took almost four months to install.

Streatham High Road, *c.* 1925. These two large blocks of shops and flats were built between Kingscourt and Mount Ephraim Roads on the grounds of Norfolk House. This was the home of Christopher Gabriel, the brother of Sir Thomas Gabriel who was Lord Mayor of London in 1866. Norfolk House was a magnificent mansion with thirteen bedrooms and stood in over fifteen acres of gardens and parkland. In the grounds were numerous greenhouses, three coach houses, a stable and a lodge.

The Golden Domes, *c*. 1913. Also known as the Streatham Picture Theatre, this was the second cinema to open in Streatham and commenced business in September 1912. The management pioneered Sunday opening in the area despite strong objections by the Lord's Day Observance Society. Sunday screenings began in January 1914 with *The Vicar of Wakefield* – an ironic choice in view of the Church's strong objections to showing films on the Sabbath.

Two

Streatham Hill

Looking towards Streatham Hill from Streatham Congregational church, *c.* 1914. The development of Streatham Hill commenced in Georgian times with the erection of The Paragon. These were large villa-type properties which were built on the western side of the road, south of Brixton Hill. They were mainly occupied by wealthy families who were attracted to the rural surroundings Streatham offered while still being relatively close to London. Building continued along Streatham Hill in Victorian times, with a number of large, detached houses standing in big gardens erected here. This development received a major boost with the opening of Streatham Hill station in 1856, which made it easier for local inhabitants to commute to the city. The area quickly established a high reputation, enhanced by the building of such streets as Christchurch, Palace and Leigham Court Roads, all of which contained some of the finest property in the area.

Streatham Hill station, *c.* 1919 (above). The station was opened on 1 December 1856 by the London, Brighton and South Coast Railway (LBSCR). It was erected on the bridge over the railway lines. The building was first known as Streatham station, but when the South London and Sutton Junction Railway opened their station in 1868, just off Streatham High Road south of Gleneagle Road, the name of the station was altered to Streatham and Brixton Hill. This was amended to Streatham Hill in 1869. The building's plain design suggests that the railway company did not at first anticipate that much trade would be done here to warrant the erection of a larger station. Notwithstanding this, the structure of the bridge is such that it is unable to carry the weight of a larger, brick building and so Streatham Hill's small, semi-rural station has survived virtually unaltered over the past 150 years. The view below dates from the mid-1920s.

Leigham Court Estate, c. 1922. In 1891 the Artisans', Labourers' and General Dwelling Company acquired Leigham Court House and grounds on which they developed the Leigham Court Estate. The first part of the development comprised the shops and flats seen here which front onto Streatham Hill. The quality of the buildings and the businesses that rented the retail units did much to allay the fears of local residents that the estate would be developed with cheap, sub-standard housing for the working classes. The estate comprises a variety of different styles of property and, as can be seen above in the advertisement painted on the side of the building, houses were available at an annual rent of between £30 and £60, with maisonettes available to tenants at between £20 and £40 per annum. The project was a mammoth undertaking and with the intervention of the First World War it took thirty-seven years to complete, the last house on the estate being built in 1928.

The Locarno and Streatham Hill Theatre 1930. By the 1920s many of the leases of the large houses that had been erected along the south-western side of Streatham Hill expired and the opportunity arose for the major redevelopment of the area. From the late 1920s to the mid-1930s this part of Streatham Hill was transformed into a prestigious entertainment centre with the erection of the Locarno Dance Hall (1929), the Gaumont Palace Cinema (1932) and the Streatham Hill Theatre (1928). The view above shows the Locarno advertising the grand Armistice Ball which was held there in November 1930. For this occasion the Locarno was decorated with bunting, flags and beautiful floral displays. The Seven Royal Hindustans amazed the gathering with their spectacular tricks while Joe Gibson's Band entertained dancers with a medley of old war-time favourites such as 'It's a Long Way to Tipperary' and 'Pack Up Your Troubles in Your Old Kit Bag'.

Streatham Hill Theatre, *c.* 1930. This was one of London's largest suburban theatres with seating for 2,600 people. This made it larger than many prestigious West End houses such as the London Coliseum, Covent Garden or the Drury Lane Theatre. The foundation stone was laid on 6 September 1928 by Evelyn Laye, a popular musical comedy actress of the day. In 1926 she had married the musical actor Sonnie Hale, who used to live with his parents at 53 Drewstead Road. He was to appear with Jessie Matthews in the theatre's opening show, *Wake Up and Dream*. Evelyn and Sonnie's marriage was to be short-lived and ended in divorce when Ms Laye discovered that her husband was having an affair with Jessie Matthews. The Theatre was badly damaged in the war and did not reopen until 1950. Over the following decade, as television became increasingly popular, audiences declined and the theatre closed in June 1962 after which it was converted into a bingo hall.

Streatham Hill College, *c.* 1932. This college was founded by Ernest Blackwell at no. 35 Streatham Hill in 1895. The building was a large imposing square Georgian house built around 1826. In January 1904 Mr Francis A. Welch took over the establishment and under his headship it continued to flourish, providing education for 'the sons of gentlemen'. The school was a typical prep school of its day providing education for young boys preparing to enter public schools, the professions and commercial life. Over the years it passed through the hands of a number of different owners and despite the difficulties caused by the First World War the college continued to prosper and acquired the adjoining property at no. 33 Streatham Hill to accommodate its growing roll of pupils. The college closed in 1936 when the buildings were demolished to make way for the erection of 'Corner Fielde', a large block of luxury flats.

London County Council tram depot, Streatham Hill, *c.* 1914. The above view shows the entrance to the depot which was built opposite Telford Avenue in 1905. In 1870 a horse tram commenced service between Kennington and Brixton and this was converted to use cable traction in 1892. At this time the London Tramways Company extended the line to Streatham Hill. To accommodate the trams, and provide a home for the winding gear, the company built a cable-car shed and power house at Streatham Hill. After the LCC took over the running of the trams it was decided to replace the cable system with electric power. As a consequence the old facilities were no longer required at Streatham Hill and they were demolished to make way for the building seen below. The trams were taken out of service in Streatham on 7 April 1951 and the tram depot was subsequently pulled down and Brixton Hill bus garage erected on the site.

33

Streatham Hill, *c.* 1912. Until the 1930s much of the northern part of Streatham Hill retained its semi-rural aspect as the road here still contained many large houses, in the front gardens of which stood large trees providing a very welcome splash of greenery. Until the Second World War some of these properties remained in single occupancy, a number being used as surgeries by local doctors and dentists. After the Second World War some of these houses were converted into flats and bedsits. By the 1960s a number of these buildings had fallen into a bad state of repair and over the years these were demolished to make way for the erection of flats and modern retail outlets. The view below shows the entrance to the Telford Park Estate at Telford Avenue. At the junction of the road is the advertising hoarding for the estate which stood here for many years until it was removed when the road was widened.

Streatham Hill looking towards Brixton Hill, *c.* 1912. On the left of the upper photograph the houses which formed the Streatham Paragon development are hidden from view behind the trees and shrubs which stand in their front gardens. The Crown and Sceptre public house (below) has stood at the junction of Streatham Hill and Streatham Place since 1822 when it was erected here for Michael Wood. In 1838 Matthew Ball operated his horse-drawn Paragon bus service to and from the City of London from the pub. A large stable building stood adjacent to the inn and was used by Ball to house his horses. This building was subsequently demolished and was replaced by an off-licence which later was incorporated into the pub. Norman Hartnell, the Queen's dressmaker, was born here in 1901 when his father was the landlord. In 1977 Norman was knighted for his services to the fashion industry and became the first couturier to be so honoured.

Streatham Hill Congregational church, *c.* 1912. This church was erected in 1871 on the summit of Brixton Hill, 300ft above the Thames, placing it level with the foot of the cross on the dome of St Paul's Cathedral. The church replaced a small union chapel which was set up here in 1829 to accommodate both Anglicans and Nonconformists living in the neighbourhood. The church was pulled down in 1982 and in 1993 the Brixton Hill United Reformed church was built on the site.

Three
Streatham Streets

View of Streatham from Leigham Court Road, c. 1919. In the years following the First World War open fields and pasture land were still to be found in and around Streatham, providing the area with pockets of rural charm. On the slopes of Leigham Court Road horses still grazed on the lush grassland which, within the space of a couple of decades, would be covered with houses. From the last quarter of the nineteenth century onwards Streatham's fields were steadily covered with roads and houses. This continual erosion of the locality's countryside was temporarily suspended during the First World War but as the country recovered and entered the 'roaring Twenties' builders resumed activity and a new wave of development commenced. Note the spires of Streatham Methodist church, the church of the English Martyrs and St Leonard's, which punctuate the skyline and were prominent local landmarks.

Abercairn Road, *c.* 1933. This road links the north-eastern and north-western ends of the Streatham Vale estate and was laid out in the 1920s. It was originally known as Aberfoyle Road but was renamed in 1923. The road backs onto land once used as railway sidings. This was formerly the site of a rifle range used by the local volunteers. Part of this land became Lambeth's first nature reserve in 1995 and the birch woodland there now provides a quiet haven for local wildlife.

Aberfoyle Road, *c.* 1933. Named after the village on the River Laggan in central Scotland commemorated by Scott in *Rob Roy*, this road dates from the early 1920s. A former resident was Albert Simner who lived at no. 39. He was pianist to the famous music hall star, Kate Carney, known affectionately as 'The Cockney Sweetheart'. She started her career at the age of ten and was still performing when in her late seventies. She died at 38 Palace Road (see p. 92) in 1950 aged eighty.

Amesbury Avenue, *c.* 1912. Laid out on the Leigham Court Estate in 1891, this road is named after the town on the River Avon in the south-eastern corner of Salisbury Plain. The musical actress May Etheridge lived at no. 76. She started her theatrical career in 1905 when, at the age of thirteen, she appeared in *The New Aladdin* at the Gaiety Theatre. She moved from her home here in 1913 after her marriage to Lord Edward Fitzgerald, the fifth son of the Duke of Leinster. Ballroom dancers Larry and Phyllis Dodge were also residents of this road and represented England on three occasions in amateur competitions. In 1957 they became Surrey Professional Ballroom Champions after being runners up in 1955 and 1956. In 1912 a Miss Cameron established the Streatham branch of the National League for Opposing Women Suffrage at her home at no. 87 Amesbury Avenue.

Baldry Gardens c. 1912. This road was originally to be called Hebburn Gardens but this name was rejected by the Metropolitan Board of Works who suggested Baldry Gardens without giving any reason for their decision. The parents of the famous aviator, Sir Alan Cobham, lived at no. 59. Sir Alan was an early pioneer of long distance flying for which he established many world records which earned him his knighthood. He later toured the UK with his famous flying circus.

Barcombe Avenue, c. 1919. Ivy is gradually engulfing these houses at the junction with Emsworth Street. Barcombe Avenue was laid out on the Leigham Court Estate in 1891 and was named after a small village three miles north of Lewes in East Sussex. The development was commonly known as the ABCD Estate after the initial letters of the four roads running east from Streatham Hill, called Amesbury, Barcombe, Cricklade and Downton Avenues.

Barcombe Avenue, *c.* 1912. This road was built by the Artisans', Labourers' and General Dwelling Company which developed the Leigham Court Estate with good quality housing that it let at competitive rents. A tragic discovery was made here in April 1903 by Archibald Dewdney of Hambro Road. When walking down Barcombe Avenue he noticed a small brown paper parcel lying on the step of one of the houses. On examining the package he discovered that it contained the dead body of a small child. Sadly it was not uncommon at the time for babies to die shortly after birth. Many poor people could not afford the cost of burial so they would leave the body in a public place where discovery was assured, knowing that the corpse would receive a Christian burial at public expense. There are numerous reports of such discoveries taking place throughout Streatham prior to the First World War.

Barrow Road, *c.* 1919. Until 1884 this road was called Bakers Lane. Prior to this it was known as Burton's Lane or Pasture Road as it led to the fields lying on this side of the High Road. These originally formed part of Burton's Farm which in the 1760s comprised around 95 acres. The top view shows the ancient weatherboarded cottages that stood at the High Road end of the street. The southernmost of these old houses was for many years occupied by William Bryant, who was born here in 1853. His father was the first lamplighter for Streatham and each evening would tour the parish on his horse, lighting the old gas lamps that use to illuminate the town. In the early hours of the morning he would then retrace his steps and, to save dismounting from his steed, would extinguish the lamps with a long stick while the horse rode by. The cottages were demolished in the mid-1930s to make way for Sanders House which now occupies this site.

Braxted Park, *c.* 1912. When this road was laid out in 1902 it was originally known as Braxted Road but was renamed in 1906 to commemorate the estate of the landowner, Charles H. Copley Du Cane of Braxted Park, in Witham, Essex. The road was developed by Hill & Tyler, builders, who promoted the road as 'an ideal situation for a suburban residence'. Much emphasis was given to the road's close proximity to Streatham Common and the neighbourhood was referred to as 'Healthy Streatham'. The developers boasted that each house had a garden of sufficient size 'so that a full-sized badminton court or small-size croquet or tennis court can be laid out if desired'. Prospective purchasers were advised that every house erected here had a 'grand entrance hall measuring 26ft 6in by 10ft which, with its cosy corners and handsome fireplace and fittings, is suitable for use as an extra reception room, smoking lounge, or afternoon tea room'.

Bridgewood Road, *c.* 1928. Railway sleepers formed the surface of Bridgewood Road when this photograph was taken shortly after the street had been completed in the mid 1920s. At no. 14 lived Stanley Gibbs, a will-known member of the local scout troop. In October 1933 he saw a woman fall into the River Thames from the steps by Cleopatra's Needle on the Embankment. He dived in after her and dragging her to the bank tried desperately to revive her but without success. For his bravery he was awarded the Bronze Cross by the Chief Scout, Lord Baden Powell.

Broadview Road, *c.* 1933. This street was laid out in 1923. In 1949 it was the home of Arthur 'Dicky' Whittington, a twenty-year-old press photographer. That year he became the youngest ever prize-winner of the *Encyclopedia Britannica* British News Pictures of the Year Competition. His award in the features section was for his photograph of 'Mother and Children', portraying a lioness and her two cubs which was taken on his first assignment for the *Illustrated* magazine.

Broxholm Road, *c.* 1912. This road was developed between Leigham Court Road and Royal Circus from 1899 onwards and is lined by large late Victorian and Edwardian houses. For many years this street was the home of one of Streatham's best-loved and respected members of the Scouts, Charles Hare. Known affectionately by generations of scouters as 'Bun', he joined the 2nd Streatham Hill Scout Group attached to Christ Church in 1932. For the next sixty-five years he was to dedicate his life to the movement and he was awarded the Silver Acorn, one of the Scouts' highest service awards, for his work with the organization. In a period of fifty years he never missed a single summer camp. During his lifetime with the scouts he served as scout master and finally as group secretary. He died in April 1997 aged seventy-nine.

Buckleigh Road, *c.* 1917. The most famous resident of this road is probably James Bond, British Agent 007, in the form of the actor Roger Moore. While attending RADA Roger met Lucy Woodard, who later changed her name to Doorn Van Steyn. They married in 1946 and lived with Lucy's parents at no. 16 Buckleigh Road before moving to Wavertree Court in Streatham Hill. Their marriage ended in 1952 after Roger's affair with the singer Dorothy Squires whom he married in 1953.

Canmore Gardens, *c.* 1933. This street of sedate mid-1920s houses seems an unlikely home for a Time Lord, but Dr Who spent the first ten years of his life here in the form of the actor Peter Davison. Peter attended the nearby primary school in Granton Road until his father purchased a business in Surrey and the family moved to Woking. Peter is also well known for his role as Tristan Farnham, the young student vet, in the television drama *All Creatures Great and Small.*

Carnforth Road, *c.* 1933. This road dates from 1923 and is named after the town on Morecambe Bay, seven miles north of Lancaster. Matilda Exall, one of Streatham's oldest residents, lived at no. 19 where she celebrated her 101st birthday in July 1949. She was born in Kennington in 1848 and could hear the applause from the Oval Cricket Ground from her house. She remembered how as a young child she met many of the cricketers who played at the Oval who were frequent guests at her parents' home. She married a direct descendant of John Carver, leader of the Pilgrim Fathers who sailed for New England in 1620 and was the first Governor of the Plymouth Colony. Matilda moved to Carnforth Road in 1924 from which time she was a regular worshipper at the Baptist church in Mitcham Lane. As a young child she was the weakest member of her family and was often told by her mother that she would 'never make old bones'.

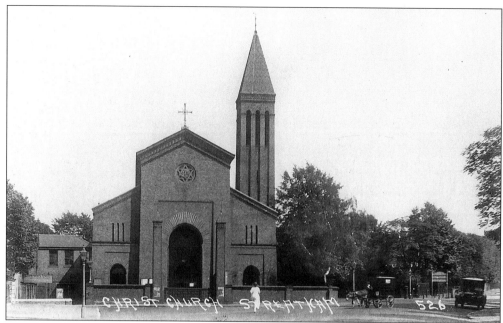

Christ Church, c. 1912. Designed by James Wild in 1841 this is one of the architectural gems of Streatham and is a Grade I listed building. The design was prompted by the Rector of Streatham, the Revd Henry Blunt, who, having recently been in Italy, mentioned to Wild how impressed he was by some of the small twelfth-century churches he saw there. These remarks encouraged the architect to design Christ Church in a similar style.

Christchurch Road, c. 1919. The bell tower of Christ Church stands 113ft high and dominates the skyline at the junction of Streatham Hill and the South Circular Road. This street forms part of the Roupell Park Estate and links the northern part of Streatham Hill with Tulse Hill. The road was originally lined with large detached Victorian residences with extensive gardens which provided comfortable homes for wealthy merchants and successful businessmen.

Christchurch Road, *c.* 1919. One of the most entertaining residents of this street was the famous conjurer James Bassett who died at his home at no. 41 Christchurch Road in 1907 aged fifty-three. He performed under the stage name of Charles Bertram and took up conjuring after a business dispute left him penniless. He made his first appearance on the stage in 1885. James had a natural flare for card tricks and within a short period of time had established himself as Britain's leading conjurer and 'card manipulator'. He appeared before members of the royal family on over twenty occasions and also performed in front of the Shah of Persia at Waddesdon Manor at the invitation of Baron de Rothschild. James was also a gifted marksman and in 1869 took part in the Tir International event in Brussels with the 'Riflemen of England' where he won several first prizes and received a commemorative medal from King Leopold I. He is buried in West Norwood Cemetery.

Conyers Road, *c.* 1924. This street was the home of two remarkable sisters, the Misses Ruby and Mabel Polkingshorne. Following the First World War they began writing educational books for children and by the late 1950s had produced over forty titles covering geography, history, arithmetic and English. Their books were used in schools all over the world and were published in seventeen languages. Because they were shy and reclusive, few local residents knew of their fame except for the postman who must have wondered why so many children from around the world used to write to them.

Copley Park, *c.* 1912. This road was laid out on the Streatham Lodge Estate in 1906. It is named after Charles H. Copley Du Cane of Braxted Park, Witham, Essex, who owned the freehold of the land. His mother's maiden name was Copley and her father was Baron Lyndhurst. In the 1920s, Percy Hollingsworth, who lived at no. 5, won six awards in the *Daily Telegraph* competition for London and suburban gardens, winning the £100 first prize in 1923.

Criffel Avenue, *c.* 1919. This road dates from 1881 and is named after a hill and prominent landmark three miles south of New Abbey in Dumfries and Galloway. This formed part of the Scottish estate of Martin and Marianne Stewart who were the landowners here. William Newton Bakewell, the contractor's engineer for the building of the Forth Bridge, lived at no. 41 Criffle Avenue and died there in November 1913 aged sixty-eight.

The British Home and Hospital for Incurables, Crown Lane, *c.* 1912. This imposing gateway forms the entrance to the British Home and Hospital for Incurables which was opened by the Prince and Princess of Wales on 3 July 1894. This was an occasion of much celebration in Streatham. Shops and houses along the royal route were decorated with flags and bunting and large crowds lined the roads to cheer and welcome the royal party.

The British Home and Hospital for Incurables, Crown Lane, *c.* 1912. In 1861, at a meeting chaired by the Lord Mayor of London, Sir William Cubitt, a group of businessmen agreed that 'an institution be established for the relief of incurable diseases, accident or deformity'. Two years later a home was opened near Clapham Common to bring their aims into effect. After thirty years the need for a larger building became pressing and it was decided to relocate the home to purpose-built premises at Streatham. Since the home opened here in 1894 there have been many additions to the original building, including the chapel, seen below. In 1912 the Alexandra Wing was added and named in honour of Edward VII's Queen, the home's patron. To celebrate the Hospital's centenary a public appeal was launched which raised £2 million so that a further wing could be built, which was opened in 1996.

Daysbrook Road, *c.* 1912. The large building between the houses is the Streatham Hill and Clapham High School for Girls which was built in Wavertree Road in 1895. The school was badly damaged when a V1 bomb fell at the junction of Daysbrook and Wavertree Roads at midnight on 27 July 1944. The civil defence units successfully rescued two people from the debris of 12 Daysbrook Road but sadly Charles Kerbey was killed by the bomb which wrecked his house at 23 Wavertree Road.

Donnybrook Road, *c.* 1933. Number 3 was the boyhood home of Major Archibald Pagan of the Royal Signals. As an eighteen-year-old member of the Home Guard he received a special commendation for helping to rescue six people from bomb-damaged houses in Babington Road. In 1940 he enlisted in the Royal Signals and spent most of the war in Burma. He decided to make the army his career and in 1958 was awarded the MBE for his service in Malaya during the emergency there.

Downton Avenue, *c.* 1924. This road was laid out on the Leigham Court Estate in 1891 and is named after a village six miles south of Salisbury. The artist John Doman Turner moved to no. 63 in 1912 where he lived until his death in 1938. He was a stockbroker's clerk who developed his artistic skills through a correspondence course. A founder member of the Camden Town group of painters, his work can be seen today in a number of public collections including the Courtauld Institute.

Drewstead Road, *c.* 1912. This street was known as Leigham Court Road West until 1903 when it adopted its new name in honour of Beriah Drew, Lord of the Manor of Leigham from 1836 to 1878. Beriah was one of the most influential residents of Streatham and had extensive land holdings in the parish. He was described as being an old-fashioned man, always dressed in black, with a cadaverous-looking face. He died on 17 August 1878 aged ninety and is buried in St Leonard's churchyard.

54

Drewstead Road, c. 1912. A former resident of this street was Thomas Eckersley, a famous poster artist. He studied art at the Salford Art School and in 1935 moved to London where he commenced his career as a free-lance poster artist and illustrator. During the war he served in the RAF. However, despite this he continued to draw, producing the logo for war-time savings posters and a series of accident prevention posters which were displayed in factories throughout the UK. He was also responsible for designing the weathercock which featured on posters promoting the extension of the Underground's Central Line. In addition to his work in the public sector he also produced material for commercial companies, including the design of Neptune which helped boost the sale of cod liver oil after the war. In the 1949 New Year's Honours he was awarded the OBE and was the first poster artist to receive such an award.

Ellison Road, *c.* 1912. This street was the site of one of the largest private collections of exotic tropical plants in the UK. These were cultivated by Ernest Hepworth and by 1956 he had over 25,000 plants in his huge greenhouse here. This was a popular local attraction, not only for the banana and grapefruit trees it contained, but also for its wildlife, including tree-hopping frogs and a large toad that was transported around the greenhouse in a truck along a miniature railway line.

Estreham Road, *c.* 1912. This road originally formed an extension of Ellison Road but was renamed Estreham Road in 1911. Estreham is the name by which Streatham is recorded in the Domesday survey of 1086. During the Zeppelin raid on Streatham on the night of 23 September 1916 a bomb fell opposite the railway station, completely wrecking nos. 10-13. Mrs Mary Chadwick of no. 12 was killed in the blast and it took firemen two hours to rescue her daughter from the rubble.

Streatham Common station, Estreham Road, *c.* 1912. The first station here was opened by the London, Brighton and South Coast Railway on 1 December 1862 when it was known as Greyhound Lane station. The name was changed to Streatham Common in 1870. The original building was demolished when the larger station seen here was erected on the site in 1903.

Estreham Road Drill Hall, *c.* 1912. This was the HQ for Streatham's local Territorial unit which formed A Company of the 5th East Surrey Regiment and subsequently the 225th Anti-Tank Battery, Royal Artillery. By the mid 1950s the hall was no longer required by the TA and in 1958 it was acquired by the orthodox Jewish community in Streatham who converted it into a synagogue. Since 1983 it has been used by local Muslims as the Hayderi Islamic Centre.

Fallsbrook Road, *c*. 1919. On Guy Fawkes night in 1983 local residents had a firework display here that they had not planned when the local Italian ice cream factory run by the Dodman family was the scene of a gigantic explosion. Such was the force of the blast people walking in the street nearby were blown to the ground and windows in the surrounding houses were shattered. Fortunately the Dodmans were out at the time of the explosion and no one was seriously injured by the blast.

Fernwood Avenue, *c*. 1924. To many readers of daily newspapers Fernwood Road would be a familiar address for it was from his home here that Capt. Neil Dewar kept up a steady correspondence to the editors of the nation's press. By 1970 he had an estimated 4,000 letters published in over fifty different newspapers. His unusual hobby began when he was in hospital and was bet £5 that he could not get a letter published in a newspaper; a wager he readily accepted and easily won.

Gleneagle Road, c. 1919. This road was laid out in 1867 and is named after the glen in Blackford parish in Perthshire, famous for its golf course. Among the former residents of this road was Fred Beckwith, a famous continental jockey, who retired here in 1946. In 1895 he was a page boy in a Folkestone hotel where a number of French racehorse owners used to stay when visiting Britain. Noting his height of only 4ft 6in, one of them suggested that he go to France and train as a jockey. This he did and quickly discovered he had a natural gift for racing and was soon riding for some of the leading stables in France and Italy. Fred won many important continental races, including the Prix de Lombardia, the Italian equivalent of the British Two Thousand Guineas. During the Second World War he was interned by the Germans following which he returned to England and spent a happy retirement in Gleneagle Road.

The Broadway, Gleneagle Road, *c.* 1928. The shops situated between Gleneagle Road and Streatham Green were built in 1884 and were originally known as the Broadway. At no. 18 Mrs Knights ran a florist's business. In 1901 she fashioned a magnificent display of blooms into a 6ft high model of Sir Thomas Lipton's yacht, *Shamrock II*, which she presented to him as a good-luck gesture on his departure from England to compete in the Americas Cup races off the US coast.

Gleneldon Road, *c.* 1912. No. 16 Gleneldon Road was the home of Leslie Grimwood who was arrested in May 1914 for inciting a crowd of 300 people against a group of suffragettes who were holding a meeting on Streatham Common. It was clear where the magistrate's sympathies lay as he dismissed the charges without even hearing the defence. He justified Leslie's actions by saying 'the behaviour of the suffragists had created a strong feeling of resentment among the crowd'.

Glenister Park Road, c. 1933. This street was the home of the women's high jump world record holder, Sheila Lerwill. A gifted netball player, Sheila's interest in jumping began when her boyfriend took her to Tooting Bec athletics track. In August 1950 she became the European women's high jump champion and in 1951 the world champion, with a record-breaking jump of 5 feet $7\frac{5}{8}$ inches. Sheila won the silver medal for Britain in the Helsinki Olympics in 1952.

Grayscroft Road, c. 1933. This street was developed in the mid 1920s and the road here was still a muddy track when this photograph was taken. The street appears to have been named after an ancient field which formed part of the manor of Streatham and Tooting Bec in the thirteenth century. The name 'croft' signifies an enclosed area of land adjacent to a dwelling house which was farmed by the occupier to provide food or used as pasture for livestock.

The Greyhound public house, *c.* 1925. An inn has occupied this site at the top of Greyhound Lane from at least the early 1720s and probably earlier. The pub seen here was built in 1871 for its new owner Edwin Janes. He came from Hoxton in Middlesex and his family were long time licensees at the Greyhound. Note the statue of a greyhound sitting over the main entrance to the pub. The building shown here was demolished in 1930 when the present-day pub was erected on the site.

Greyhound Lane, *c.* 1912. This is one of the ancient trackways of Streatham which led to an area of deserted wasteland called Lonesome, on the parish border with Mitcham. Few people would venture along the lane at night as Lonesome was considered a dangerous place to linger alone, being inhabited by gipsies and tramps. The opening of Streatham Common railway station in 1862 encouraged builders to erect the large houses which front the road between the station and Streatham High Road. These provided comfortable homes for the influx of new residents in the closing decades of the nineteenth century who were attracted to the area by its close proximity to the railway station. However, the western end of Greyhound Lane, which now forms Streatham Vale, was considered unsuitable for building due to the bad reputation Lonesome had developed over the years and remained undeveloped until the 1920s.

Greyhound Lane, *c*. 1912. This row of shops stands on the north-western side of the Estreham Road junction with Greyhound Lane and use to be known as Station Terrace. Note the large oil jars fixed either side of the first floor windows of no. 5. These were placed there as an advertising feature either by William Stevens, who occupied the premises in 1888, or by the Buxton brothers who moved in shortly thereafter. They were both oilmen selling a range of household goods.

The Railway Hotel, Greyhound Lane, *c.* 1912. This pub stands on the eastern corner of Ellison Road and dates from the late 1860s. The building was started by a Mr Blenkarn who probably anticipated an influx of residents to the area following the opening of the railway station in 1862. However, when this did not occur he abandoned the building and it stood unfinished for almost twenty years. It was finally completed in 1879 when Richard Dootson became the first publican here.

Greyhound Lane. Immanuel Church Mission Room stands at the junction with Pathfield Road. This was erected in 1899 and replaced a large wooden hut on wheels that use to occupy this site. The hut was used as a chapel by the Baptists who pushed it to wherever they could find a local farmer who was prepared to let it stay on his land. The hut finally came to rest here in the 1790s and ceased to be used as a chapel when the Baptists built their church in Lewin Road in 1877.

St Andrew's church, Guildersfield Road, c. 1912. Designed by local architect Sir Ernest George, St Andrew's was built in 1886 as a memorial to the life of the Revd Stenton Eardley (see p. 12). During the Second World War local fire-watchers used the church tower as an observation post. A fire completely gutted the church in the early hours of 10 March 1992 and the site is now occupied by housing, including at no. 51a the new vicarage for the incumbent of Immanuel church.

Hailsham Avenue. *c.* 1912. Developed from 1891 onwards, this road is named after the small market town situated seven miles north of Eastbourne in East Sussex. A former resident of this road was Wing-Cdr Alec Cranmer who was one of the youngest members of the Royal Flying Corps in the First World War. He served with the RAF in the Second World War and was demobbed with the rank of Acting Wing Commander. Alec and his wife, Constance, were both keen tennis players and they founded the Fairfield Tennis Club at Streatham Hill in 1923. The club's original headquarters was in a large house with a big garden that stood on the site of Streatham Hill Theatre, now the Megabowl (see p. 31). The club was successful in finding a new ground and subsequently played on courts at Briar Avenue in Norbury.

Helmsdale Road, *c.* 1933. This road was laid out on the Streatham Vale Estate in 1925 and was named after the village and river on the east coast of the Highlands of Scotland. One of Streatham's worse V1 flying bomb incidents of the Second World War occurred here when a bomb fell in the River Graveney on 22 June 1944. The explosion claimed ten lives, with five people being killed in nos 46-50 Sherwood Avenue and five in nos 27-31 Woodmansterne Road.

Heybridge Avenue, *c.* 1912. For over fifty years the sisters Bertha and Julia Munsey ran Lexden House School in their home at no. 10. The Whittington sisters helped them; Ruth always wore blue clothes while her sister, Ivy, dressed in brown. The kindergarten was held in the large first-floor front room. The older children were taught in the downstairs rear room where the desks, made by the Munseys' brother, were arranged to accommodate twenty pupils. Following the death of Bertha in 1953 Julia, then aged eighty-five, reluctantly retired and the school closed.

Hillside Road, c. 1914. In June 1915 a large 'Patriotic Rally' was held on waste ground here, located at the top of Wavertree Road and Downton Avenue. Around 2,000 local inhabitants attended the gathering at which it was announced that the 13th East Surrey Rifles were being formed in Wandsworth and recruiting would commence at once to raise a company of Streatham men for the unit. The meeting closed with loud cheering and the National Anthem was sung.

Holmwood Gardens, c. 1914. This street formed part of a private development to the north of Christ Church which was laid out between 1895 and 1899. It was designed by Charles Joseph Bentley and an attractive feature of the road was the large area of gardens around which the houses were built. Many of the dwellings here were constructed by the Stringer family and were built to a high standard making the property much sought after.

Hopton Road, *c.* 1914. Harry George Stride lived in Beechcroft Mansions here. In 1920 he started work at the Royal Mint as an Executive Officer and steadily rose to a senior position within the organization. He was responsible for organizing the arrangements for the withdrawal of Britain's silver coinage and its replacement with cupro-nickel coins, a project for which he was awarded the OBE in the King's 1951 Birthday Honours.

Kempshott Road, *c.* 1914. One of the earliest residents of this road was Sir Thomas Cave-Brown-Cave who lived here from the early 1870s until 1880. He was educated at Repton and during the Crimean War he entered the War Office where he initially worked without pay. He subsequently rose through the organization to retire in 1900 as Deputy Accountant-General of the Army. For over twenty years he also served as a Commissioner of the Royal Hospital, Chelsea.

Keymer Road, *c.* 1912. This road was probably named after the Kymer (a.k.a. Keymer) family who were large landowners in Streatham. Mrs Mary Ann Kymer and her daughter Elizabeth built a girls' school in Mitcham Lane in 1831 which was known as the 'Blue School'. In 1837 Elizabeth gave the Streatham School Society a plot of land on which St Leonard's Boys' School was built and later handed over to the society the management of her girls' school (see p. 84).

Killieser Avenue, *c.* 1914. This road was laid out in 1881 and was named after part of the Scottish estate of the landowners, Marianne and Martin Stewart. The parents of the noted UK and USA play producer, Reginald Denham, lived at no. 2. Between 1918 and 1940 Reginald produced eighty-six plays including *The Moon and Sixpence*, *After Dark*, *Such Men Are Dangerous*, and *To What Red Hell*. He was also co-author of *Give Me Yesterday*, *Ladies In Retirement* and *Suspect*.

Kingscourt Road, *c.* 1914. One of this roads most famous former residents was the popular 1950s wrestler Johnny 'Drop-Kick' Peters. During his career, which involved well over 2,000 contests, he displaced his collar bone five times, broke the same ankle twice, dislocated both his shoulders and had twenty-seven stitches in his tongue. He wrestled all round the world and while visiting Malaya, when serving with the Royal Navy, won the country's Welter and Middleweight Championship.

Kirkstall Gardens, *c.* 1930. Kirkstall is the name of the Scottish estate of the Stewart family who were the landowners of the Telford Park Estate. The road was developed between Kirkstall Road and New Park Road in the mid-1920s. Before the houses were erected here the land was occupied by a small pig farm, the smell of which did not endear the establishment to the local residents.

Leigham Avenue, c. 1914. The Streatham Manor Nursing Home was based at nos. 11-13 Leigham Avenue and it was here that the actress Patricia Plunkett was born on 17 December 1926. She trained at RADA and while appearing as Juliet in their production of *Romeo and Juliet* she was spotted by a theatrical agent who sent her for an audition which led to a part in *Stage Door*. Her next appearance on the West End stage was to make her a star when she played the title role in *Pick-Up Girl* at the Prince of Wales Theatre in 1946. This production was seen by Queen Mary and her praises brought Pat a great deal of celebrity at the time. Patricia later joined the famous Rank Charm School which led to her appearing in a number of films, including *Mandy* with Jack Hawkins, *For Them That Trespass* with Richard Todd and *It Always Rains on Sunday*. Manor Court now stands on the site of the nursing home, in which building the mother of the band leader Ray Noble once lived.

Leigham Court Road, *c.* 1914. The Manor of Leigham was purchased by Beriah Drew in 1836 and he subsequently laid out Leigham Court Road through his new estate which he developed with large Victorian houses (see p. 54). A few of the original houses survive today to provide an indication of the grandness of the properties that once lined this road. Some of the early houses here were built by the Trollope family and Joseph Harvey Trollope lived at no. 10 (Barham House) from 1861 to 1868, after which he moved to no. 16, Woodlawn, which is currently used as the Streatham Darby and Joan Club. George Francis Trollope, the head of the family, resided for over thirty years at Elmfield (no. 34) and died there in 1895. He and his wife are buried in St Leonard's churchyard. The family's building company later merged to become Trollope and Colls, which today forms part of the Trafalgar House Group.

Leigham Court Road, c. 1914. George Chirgwin, the famous music-hall artiste who styled himself 'The White-eyed Kaffir' lived at Easedale, no. 9, the site of which is now covered by shops at the Streatham Hill end of the road. George was born in 1854 and first appeared on the stage in 1861. He originally teamed up with his brother Jack in a minstrel act known as the Brothers Chirgwin. His solo career started by accident when his brother was unable to perform one night and George appeared by himself. He continued his double act, finally breaking away in 1878, after which he performed solo for the next thirty years, often giving up to six performances a night and earning as much as £100 a week. George was a talented musician and could play the violin, cello, piano, banjo and the bagpipes! He later moved to The Laurels, no. 1 Polworth Road, where he died in November 1922 aged sixty-seven. St Peter's church, below, stands at the junction of Glennie Road (see p. 76).

St Peter's church, Leigham Court Road, *c.* 1914. Richard Drew, the grandson of Beriah Drew, was the architect of this church which was opened in 1870. Later additions were undertaken in 1886/87 to the designs of George Fellowes Prynne. The church was the first in Streatham to have a memorial to Queen Victoria when, in May 1901, its large stained glass window was unveiled by the Bishop of Southwark. St Peter's has an imposing façade and is a Grade II* listed building.

Leigham Vale, *c.* 1914. Until 1896 this street was known as Leigham Valley Road. The man who dropped the last bomb of the Second World War lived at no. 70 Leigham Vale. He was Warrant Officer Alan Davis Rendell who flew with 110 (Hyderabad) Squadron. He was trained in Canada and initially served with Coastal Command before travelling to India in 1943 where he flew Vengeance dive-bombers and then Mosquito fighter-bombers.

Lewin Road, *c.* 1912. Robert Buchanan, the Victorian poet, novelist and dramatist died in Lewin Road on 10 June 1901. He wrote plays for the famous actress Mrs Patrick Campbell, as well as for Lillie Langtry, the favourite of King Edward VII. In 1900 he suffered a stroke while strolling along Regent Street and became bedridden. He subsequently came to Lewin Road where his sister nursed him for eight months until his death.

Lydhurst Avenue *c.* 1912. The Artisans', Labourers' and General Dwelling Company laid this road out on the Leigham Court Estate in 1891. The road runs between Faygate Road and Mount Nod/Hitherfield Roads. The houses on the northern side of the road were built over the railway tunnel which runs between Leigham Junction and Streatham Hill station.

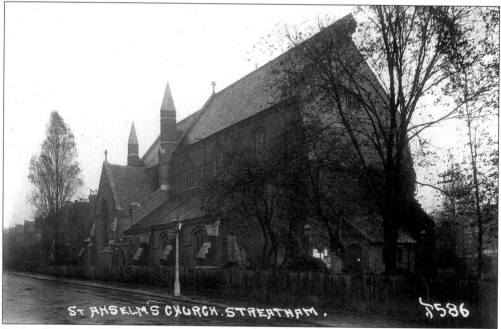

St Anselm's Church, Madeira Road, *c.* 1912. This church stood at the junction of Madeira and Oakdale Roads and was built in 1882 to serve the spiritual needs of the Coventry Park Estate. It was designed by R.J. Withers but was never fully completed. An incendiary bomb damaged the church in 1940 and later that year it suffered severe blast damage. In 1943 it was discovered that the church was in danger of collapse and it was closed and subsequently demolished.

Church of the English Martyrs, Mitcham Lane, *c.* 1919. Situated on the corner of Tooting Bec Gardens and Mitcham Lane, the Roman Catholic church of the English Martyrs is a prominent local landmark. The architect was A.E. Purdie and the church was built in 1892/93. This was the first Catholic church to be built in Streatham and was chiefly financed by Robert Measures, a wealthy businessman who lived locally and whose wife was a devout Catholic.

The altar in the church of the English Martyrs, Mitcham Lane, *c.* 1919. This altar is one of the most ornate in Streatham and stands at the western end of the church. On the rear wall, either side of the altar, are aumbries, above which are two carved heads. On the right are those of Robert Measures and his wife, Maria, and on the left their daughter and Father William Lloyd, the first rector of the church.

Mitcham Lane, *c.* 1916. Standing in the immediate foreground, in front of the Presbytery of the church of the English Martyrs, is Streatham fire station. The building was opened in December 1903 and remained in use until May 1971 when the brigade moved to a new station which was erected on the London Road in Norbury. Since 1977 the building has been used as the South London Islamic Centre.

Mitcham Lane, *c.* 1916. Until 1880 an old cottage stood on Mitcham Lane, between the Green and Streatham High Road. This was demolished when the buildings seen above were erected on the site. These were originally known as Chestnut Villas. In September 1914 the Streatham Rifle Club established their headquarters in the building closest to the Green. These houses were in their turn pulled down in 1933 when this site was redeveloped.

Mitcham Lane, c. 1912. The shops on the right of this view were built on the small front gardens of nos 19 and 21 Mitcham Lane. James Skilton ran a newsagent's business at no. 19 and newspaper placards can be seen resting against the front of his premises. His father use to work for the Rector of Streatham and his mother was a cook at Coventry House, a large mansion that stood by Streatham Common. Note the chapel of the Plymouth Brethren to the north of the shops.

Mitcham Lane, *c.* 1912. St Leonard's School is on the left. This building was erected in 1909 to replace Miss Kymer's 'Blue School' for girls and the adjacent infants' school which was built here in 1856 (see p. 71). Next to the school are two small cottages which date back to the late eighteenth or early nineteenth century. In the mid 1800s Robert Sandaver lived here. His son, James, was the village shoemaker and later went on to become the verger of Immanuel church.

Mitcham Lane, *c*. 1912. St Leonard's Boys' School stands on the eastern corner of Mitcham Lane and Ambleside Avenue. The school seen here was built in 1868 to replace the schoolroom erected in 1837 on the land donated by Miss Kymer. On the other side of the junction are the stables of Charles Sorby Straw. He was a noted horse dealer and riding master who traded horses with King Edward VII and the Prince of Siam. He died in 1921 aged fifty-eight at his home in Babington Road.

Thrale Hall Hotel, Mitcham Lane, *c*. 1912. This building dates from the 1860s and stood on the western junction of Ambleside Avenue. Originally called Thrale House, it was used as a girls' school and 'hydropathic' centre before being converted into a hotel. In 1980 the building was acquired by the Chinese Embassy who used it to accommodate their commercial and technical staff. The hotel was subsequently demolished and the site developed with housing.

Montrell Road, *c.* 1914. This road was developed between Tierney Road and Streatham Place from 1878 onwards. A former resident of this street was John Miller, who died at his home at no. 32 in October 1921 aged seventy-two. He retired here in July 1901 after a lifetime of service with the royal family at Buckingham Palace where he worked in the office of the Master of the Horse. His father, Charles Miller, was also in royal service and was the sub-comptroller of the Royal household during the reign of Queen Victoria. John Miller was born and brought up in St James's Palace where his father had an official apartment. Another resident here was the athlete Mary Lines who lived at no. 31. A noted runner in the early 1920s, she became the British ladies' 100, 220, 440 and 880 yard record holder. In September 1922 she become the 220-yard World Champion with a record-breaking sprint of 27 seconds, which she reduced a week later to 26.8 seconds.

Mount Ephraim Lane, *c.* 1914. June Whitfield, one of Britain's most popular comedy actresses, was born at 44 Mount Ephraim Lane on 11 November 1925. June's father, John Whitfield, was a Streatham member on Wandsworth Council and was appointed managing director of Dictograph Telephones Ltd in 1927. The family later moved to Calderwood (formerly The Limes), no. 5 Palace Road, which at one time was used as the vicarage for Christ Church.

Mount Ephraim Road, *c.* 1914. The famous map publisher, Edward Stanford, moved here following his marriage to Constance Hewer in February 1871 when they set up their home at Lynstead, now no. 34 Mount Ephraim Road. Edward started his business in 1852 and quickly decided to specialize in the publication and sale of maps and related items. In 1885 he became the official distributor of Ordnance Survey maps and in 1893 he received a Royal Warrant and was appointed 'Geographer to the Queen'.

Mount Nod Road, *c.* 1912. The noted engineer, John James Webster, died at his home at no. 81 Mount Nod Road on 30 October 1914 aged sixty-nine. He was born in Warrington in 1845 and had an impressive career, specializing in the construction of bridges, piers and docks. Among his commissions was the Conway Suspension Bridge, the swing bridge at Littlehampton and the Widnes-Runcorn transporter bridge as well as piers at Dover, Bangor, Minehead and Llandudno. In open competition he was placed either first or second on fourteen different occasions. He designed the gigantic wheel erected at Earls Court and the stadium and constructional work for four of the largest buildings put up at the Franco-British Exhibition. The Institution of Civil Engineers awarded him their highest honour when he was presented with the Telford Gold Medal. He is buried at West Norwood Cemetery.

New Park Road, *c.* 1933. This road was formerly known as Balams Lane and Bleakhall Lane. Until 1884 various parts of the road had subsidiary names with nos 66-70 being called Good's Cottages, nos 67-73 known as Crown Place, nos 75-89 Crown Cottages, nos 93-97 Rose Cottages and nos 101-153 Park View Cottages. In addition other parts of the road were known as Commerce Place, Park Terrace, Wallis's Cottages and Telegraph Place.

New Park Road, *c.* 1928. Jimmy Gold, one of the members of the Crazy Gang, moved to New Park Road shortly before the Second World War. The Gang was formed in 1932 and for thirty years was one of Britain's most popular comedy troupes appearing in numerous Royal Command Performances. The Crazy Gang made their last appearance on the stage in May 1962 when they completed an eighteen-month run at the Victoria Palace in *Young at Heart*. While living here he was burgled on three occasions, including Boxing Day evening in 1948 while he was performing in London. Although nothing of great value was stolen on this occasion the thieves stripped the house of drink and ransacked the rooms before making their getaway. The first telephone connected to the local exchange was located at no. 94 New Park Road, where the Revd Bernard J. Snell could boast of having Streatham 1 as his telephone number.

Norfolk House Road, *c.* 1919. This road was laid out on the grounds of Norfolk House in 1903 (see p. 25). Captain James Bell MC, of the North Staffordshire Regiment, lived at no. 66. He was awarded the Military Cross in 1917 for leading a raiding party in broad daylight. While under heavy fire, he cleared enemy dug-outs and shell craters, killing fifteen Germans and capturing eleven prisoners. In 1916 he married Essie Cregreen, a well-known soprano from the Isle of Man.

Northanger Road, *c.* 1914. This road was badly bombed in the Second World War. At the start of the Blitz in September 1940 a high explosive bomb fell at the junction with Greyhound Lane and on 16 April 1941 a bomb scored a direct hit on no. 10. Further damage was caused when a V1 landed in the gardens between Northanger and Buckleigh Roads on 3 July 1944. The houses on the left no longer exist and this area is now the site of Immanuel School, which was built here in 1977.

Palace Road, *c.* 1933. This street forms part of the Roupell Park Estate and was named after the Crystal Palace which was rebuilt on Sydenham Hill in June 1854. The road was lined with large Victorian detached houses that had extensive gardens to the rear and carriage drives to the front. The huge trees that stood in the front gardens of properties here created a pleasant rural aspect to the road which made it a popular area for wealthy people to live. Such was the size of the houses that after the First World War many were divided into flats or converted into nursing homes. On the left of the upper view can be seen part of the notice which advised visitors that this was a private road and that 'heavy traffic, funerals and hawkers' were prohibited.

Pathfield Road, *c.* 1914. This road dates from 1885 and was laid out on the orchard of Greyhound Lane Farm. This contained apple and pear trees and gooseberry, redcurrant and blackcurrant bushes which were picked for the farmer by local children at 1d a sieve. The farm was established in the late 1700s and was rented to various tenant farmers with Zachariah Grout taking it over in 1836 after which it became known as Grout's Farm. The Grout family remained here until 1888 and when Zachariah died in 1853, the farm passed to his son, on whose death in 1875 the grandson, Joseph Grout, continued the family tradition here. The farm was one of the last in Streatham to pay its tithes in kind, the corn being tied in sheaves of equal size and put in shocks of ten sheaves each. The Rector's representative would then select one shock in ten which would be transported to the Tithe Barn which stood on land now occupied by St Leonard's church hall.

Trinity Presbyterian church, Pendennis Road, *c.* 1912. This building was designed by the local architect Sir Ernest George, who was President of the Royal Institute of British Architects from 1908-1910. The building was erected in 1877 at which time there was insufficient funds available for the tower to be completed and the base was therefore roofed over. This explains the unusual shape of the building today.

Prentis Road, *c.* 1919. This road was laid out by the architect I'Anson in 1903 and formed part of the Mortimer Estate. It is named after the maiden name of Beriah Drew's wife, Elizabeth Prentis, who died in 1892. Following Beriah's death his vast land holdings in Streatham were divided between his two daughters, Maria Mortimer inheriting the land to the west of Streatham High Road, and Jane Fisher receiving the land on the eastern side of the road (see p. 84).

Rastell Avenue. The upper view dates from *c.* 1919 and that below from *c.* 1933. The street was developed in 1877 and until 1905 was known as Rastell Road. The houses here front onto Tooting Bec Common and originally stood opposite a large clay pit and brickworks which were established here to provide building material for the erection of Sternhold Avenue and the surrounding streets. When construction was completed the clay pit remained and became a large pond on which local residents would skate in the winter months. It was filled in early in the twentieth century and is now covered by the turf of the common. An ancient house known as Parson's Cottage once stood at the junction with Emmanuel Road. This was built around 1802 and later saw use as a laundry and subsequently became an unofficial refreshment house frequented by those visiting the common. It was demolished in 1901.

Ribblesdale Road, *c.* 1912. At no. 146 lived Adolphus Pullman and his wife who kept as a pet a remarkable parrot, called Esmerelda, that they taught various phrases. One night in March 1933, while the Pullmans were soundly asleep in their bed, a burglar broke into the house. Venturing into the living room the thief was startled by Esmerelda's shrill cry of 'What do you want?'. So frightened by the sudden challenge was he that the thief promptly fled from the house as the parrot continued to screech after him 'What do you want? What do you want?'.

Riggindale Road, *c.* 1912. This road was developed from 1879 onwards. George Deer, the Labour MP for Newark, moved here in 1950 to live with his married daughter. He entered Parliament in 1945 as MP for Lincoln, having served on the local council since 1922. He was Mayor of the city in 1933/34 and was appointed Sheriff of Lincoln in 1943. George was one of the most successful Labour MPs in the 1950 election, turning a Conservative majority in Newark of 1,132 into a Labour victory by 7,437 votes.

The Methodist church, Riggindale Road, *c.* 1912. This church was built in 1900 and is a Grade II listed building. It was designed in Art Nouveau style by local architect Frederick Wheeler and Edward Speed. At the time of its erection the church claimed to have the widest barrel vaulted ceiling in the country. The stained glass window in the church was the gift of Sir R. Walter Essex JP and was presented in memory of members of his family.

Rydal Road, *c.* 1912. Named after the village $1\frac{1}{2}$ miles north west of Ambleside in the Lake District, this road was laid out in 1879. Until 1906, nos 23-37 were known as Rydal Gardens (see above). These houses were built on part of the ground of the Woodlands Lawn Tennis Club. Surgeon General Maunsell CB lived at no. 3 in 1901. He was the treasurer of the Streatham Patriotic Fund which was established to raise money to provide comforts for local residents serving in the Army in the Boer War in South Africa and to relieve the suffering of their families. Another resident of this road was Serge Krish who was leader of the Krish Septet. He was a popular musician and broadcaster who rose to fame in the early 1930s through his radio work which prompted Mr Punch to write: 'Though prophets are groaning and glooming, Though trade is not all we could wish, The BBC's programmes are booming, With Melztak, Mannucil and Krish.'

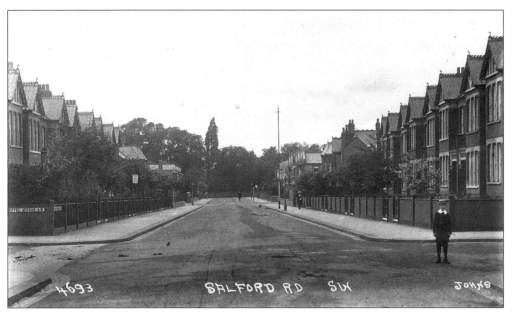

Salford Road. The upper view dates from around 1919 while that below was taken in the early 1930s. The road is named after Salford in Greater Manchester, which was the parliamentary seat of the landowner here, Mr Lees Knowles MP. The road dates from 1896 and links New Park Road with Sternhold Avenue. Number 11 Salford Road was the home of Alexander Grant. A journalist by profession, Alexander started his career in Edinburgh. In 1899 he moved south to London and was employed in Fleet Street, later becoming a member of the Press Gallery in the Houses of Parliament. In 1918 he was appointed Superintendent of Publicity for the Ministry of Pensions and was responsible for organizing the King's Fund for the Disabled which assisted wounded and injured servicemen from the First World War. In 1920 he was awarded the OBE for his work with the Fund.

Stanthorpe Road, *c.* 1912. This road was developed on the Bedford Park Estate by George Pratt in 1881. George established Streatham's first department store which carried his name and was the largest retailer in the area. He named the road after his youngest son and eleventh child, Stanley Thorpe Pratt, who was born on 26 October 1874. Thorpe was the maiden name of George's wife, Mary, who was governess to the daughter of Lady Key who lived in the Rookery, a large house which stood at the top of Streatham Common (see p. 122).

Sternhold Avenue, *c.* 1914. The actress Patricia Hayes was born at no. 128a (now no. 209) in 1909. She attended St Andrew's Convent School at Coventry Hall, Streatham Common and from an early age was keen on the stage. She won the RADA Gold Medal at the age of eighteen and initially pursued a successful stage career. However, she is best remembered today as a television comedy actress and appeared with many of the country's leading comedians including Ted Ray, Tony Hancock, Benny Hill and Arthur Haynes. She was awarded the OBE in 1988 and died in 1998 aged eighty-eight.

Streatham Place, c. 1933. This peaceful, tree-lined residential street now forms part of London's South Circular Road which is one of the busiest highways in the area. Little remains of the road seen here; what Hitler did not destroy during the Blitz was swept away by the Ministry of Transport when the road was widened in the early 1960s.

Streatham Vale, c. 1928. Formerly known as Greyhound Lane, or Lonesome Lane, this road was developed in the 1920s when the Streatham Vale Estate was laid out. Much of the land here belonged to the Crooke, Ellison and Bates families who were the largest landowners in South Streatham. Most of the local fields here were cultivated as market gardens, the rest of the land being scrub as it was of poor quality and subject to becoming waterlogged in wet weather.

Streatham Vale, *c.* 1928. The shops seen above stand between Eardley and Aberfoyle Roads and continue to trade today. The Streatham Vale Estate quickly established itself as a popular residential area between the wars. In the 1960s this road was the home of Cathy McGowan, the popular television personality who made her name in 1963 as a presenter for the *Ready, Steady, Go* pop music programme. She was originally paid £16 a week for her appearance on the show but within three years was earning around £200 an appearance, making her one of Britain's highest paid young television presenters at that time. In 1965 she was named television star of the year in a national poll. Cathy later pursued a successful career in the fashion industry. In 1970 she married the local actor Hywell Bennett who lived in Valley Road. The wedding ceremony took place in St Bartholomew's Roman Catholic church in Ellison Road. They were later divorced.

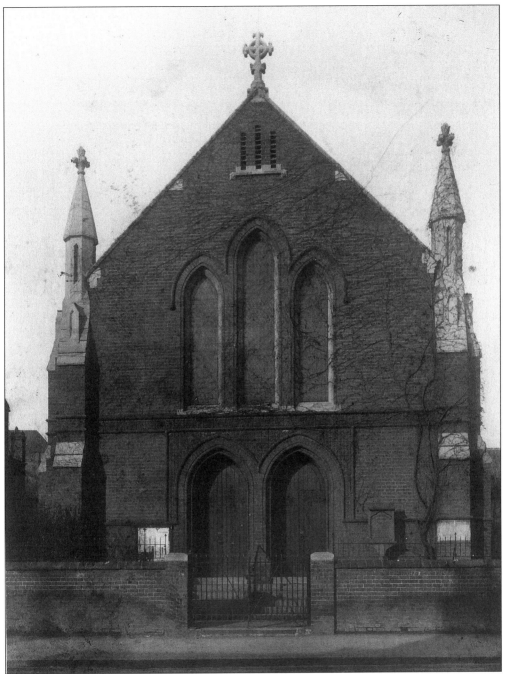

All Saints' church, Sunnyhill Road, *c.* 1912. The foundation stone of this church was laid by Archdeacon Burney on 2 July 1896. It was built as a chapel of ease to St Leonard's church and was designed by W. Newton Dunn and built by Potter Brothers of Horsham. The church was closed in 1939 but was reopened in 1944 to house the congregation of St Anselm's church (see p. 78). It was closed again in 1953 when the building became the Howland Hall which provided a venue for local community and social activities. It is now the Refuge Temple used by the Church of Our Lord Jesus Christ Apostolic Faith.

Tankerville Road, *c.* 1914. This road was developed from 1882 onwards. It is named after the Earls of Tankerville, one of whom was a patron of Surrey County Cricket Club from 1770 to 1780. Percy Roberts lived at no. 72. He was bailiff to Canon Nicholl, who was Rector of Streatham for sixty years, from 1843 to 1904. Roberts was responsible for collecting the weekly rents for the various properties the rector owned in Streatham, which included most of the houses in Shrubbery Road.

Telford Avenue, *c.* 1912. This was the main thoroughfare on the Telford Park Estate which was developed between 1878 and 1882. The land here formed part of the dowry of Sarah Kymer, the sister of Maximilian Richard Kymer, who was joint Lord of the Manor of Streatham and Tooting Bec with Richardson Borrowdaile. Sarah married Charles Telford, a city stockbroker, after whom the estate was named. Their only son, Colonel Charles Telford, died in 1894.

Telford Avenue, *c.* 1914. Probably the best-known resident of this road is the actress Linda Baron, famous for her roles as Nurse Gladys Emmanuel in the BBC television comedy programme *Open All Hours,* and as Lily-Bless-Her in *Last of the Summer Wine.* Her other TV successes have been her roles as 'aunties'; first as Auntie Pat in *The Upper Hand* and then as Auntie Mabel in the children's series *Come Outside.* Linda moved to London when she was sixteen and obtained her first stage role in a pantomime chorus line. She quickly graduated to singing in cabaret shows and appeared in revue with Sheila Hancock and Kenneth Williams. This led to her participating in the hit 1960s TV show *That Was The Week That Was* and a two year spell at the *Talk of the Town.* After raising a family in Bishop's Stortford she returned to London, first living in Camden before moving to Telford Avenue. Note the roof of St Thomas' church in the lower view (see p. 106).

St Thomas' church, Telford Avenue, *c.* 1933. The foundation stone of this church was laid on 11 May 1901 by Sir Frank Green, Lord Mayor of London, and the nave was opened for worship by the Lord Bishop of Rochester later that year, on 19 September. Before the church was built, the congregation met in a small temporary iron church which was erected in early 1885 in Telford Avenue, near the junction with Thornton Avenue. To help raise funds to finance the building of the church rents were charged for the use of pews, which varied in price from 15s to 30s a year. Emmanuel College, Cambridge, the ground landlords, agreed to donate £1,500 towards the cost of building the church on condition that one of the aisles accommodate parishioners free of charge and that the College be represented on the Board of Patronage. The practice of charging pew rents at St Thomas' was discontinued in 1937.

Tenham Avenue, *c.* 1928. At No. 17 lived Freddie Gutteridge, who for over forty years was a master at Streatham Grammar School. He joined the school in 1922 and quickly became a much-loved and highly respected member of the staff, described by many of his old pupils as 'a real life Mr Chips'. He died in 1975, aged seventy-eight, and a memorial to him was erected in the Chapel of Unity in St Leonard's church. Note the roof of St Thomas' church at the end of the road.

Thornton Avenue, *c.* 1919. The first houses were erected here in 1878 when the street was known as Thornton Road. It was not until 1884 that the part of the road between New Park Road and Sternhold Avenue was renamed Thornton Avenue. The street is named after Henry Thornton (1760-1815) who was Governor of the Bank of England and MP for Southwark. He was a member of the Clapham Sect and played an important role in campaigning for the abolition of slavery.

Thornton Avenue, *c.* 1919. Bob Willis, who later became captain of the England cricket team, shared a one-bedroom flat here with his friend Martin Tyler. They decided to move one of the single beds into the living room so they would have a room each and tossed a coin to see who would sleep where. Willis won the toss and chose the bedroom, a selection he was later to regret as the room was bitterly cold in the winter due to a lack of heating and was known by the pair as 'the fridge'. It was in November 1970, while Willis was residing in Streatham, that he received the call to join the England team in Australia to replace the injured Alan Ward. He made his debut international appearance in the Fourth Test in Sydney in January 1971 when he took the first of his 325 test wickets. In January 1984 Bob became England's leading Test wicket taker when he surpassed Freddie Trueman's record of 307 wickets by dismissing the New Zealand player B.L. Cairns in the Wellington Test match.

Thornton Road. This road runs between Kings Avenue and Thornton Avenue and was laid out by Thomas Cubitt who developed it as part of the Clapham Park Estate between 1825 and the 1860s. On the corner of Thornton Road and New Park Road stands Gothic Lodge, a Grade II listed building seen on the right in the above photograph. This house now comprises nos 138 and 140 New Park Road and was originally erected as a single dwelling in 1835. It was the home of nineteenth-century opera singers Giovanni Mario and his wife Giulia Grisi and it is reported that the great Italian composer Verdi stayed here when visiting London. One of the largest mansions to be found in Thornton Road was Cleveland House. It was purchased by Stephen Ralli in 1867 at which time 'nothing but fields and farm-gardens could be seen from the house'. The building was later used as St Winifred's Home for Girls.

Thrale Road c. 1919. This road marks the western boundary of the Streatham Park Estate which was the home of the Thrale family after whom it is named. In the latter half of the eighteenth century Streatham Park became a fashionable centre for society and here Henry Thrale and his wife, Hester, entertained the leading luminaries of the day, including David Garrick, Edmund Burke, Oliver Goldsmith, Sir Joshua Reynolds and Dr Samuel Johnson.

Tierney Road, c. 1912. This road was laid out in 1878. In December 1953 the forty-six-year-old George Mackenzie-Reid died at his home here. He and his wife, Dorothy, were noted accordion players and from the late 1930s until the time of George's death they performed a popular double act. In 1950 they entertained Princess Elizabeth and the Duke of Edinburgh aboard HMS *Surprise* in Malta and they appeared before the royal couple again in the 1953 Royal Command Performance.

A window cleaner pushes his ladders along Tierney Road in 1912.

Wavertree Road, *c.* 1914. Wasteland here was the scene of a tragic accident in 1893 when some young children were playing by the side of a large pond that stood by the road. One of them, William Pocock, aged five and a half, fell into the pond and, being unable to swim, quickly drifted into deep water. An old man minding some donkeys nearby rushed to the scene but was too late to save the child who had drowned by the time he arrived at the spot.

Furzedown College, Welham Road, *c.* 1922. Built during the First World War, Furzedown Teacher Training College quickly established a high reputation for the quality of the teachers it trained. In July 1921 Mrs Megan Lloyd George, the wife of the Prime Minister, made an official visit to Furzedown to attend the college's Speech Day. The college closed in July 1978 and the buildings are now occupied by Graveney School.

112

Westwell Road, *c.* 1922. Holland Tringham, a noted artist and illustrator, lived for a time at no. 22. He moved to Streatham in 1891 when he was at the height of his profession contributing drawings and illustrations to the leading magazines and journals of the day, such as the *Illustrated London News*. Following the death of his mother in 1899 his life entered a period of emotional turmoil. At the same time the introduction of photographic printing led to a dramatic decline in demand for his work. Sadly he sought solace in drink which resulted in a steady deterioration of his health. In early 1908 his wife, whom he had divorced in 1902, died and he went to the Isle of Man in a bid to recover from his deep despair. Once again drink got the better of him and he died in a lunatic asylum in Douglas on 26 March 1908. Ironically, in view of his intemperance, a local pub is now named in his honour and some of his drawings of old Streatham adorn its walls. Note the tower of Immanuel church on the skyline of the picture below.

Wyatt Park Road, *c.* 1928. In July 1937 a young schoolgirl called Brenda Gunner received one of the most memorable telephone calls of her life in her home at no. 75 Wyatt Park Road when the famous American crooner and film star Bing Crosby telephoned her from his Hollywood ranch. The trans-Atlantic telephone call was first prize in a film magazine competition Brenda had entered. She was a great fan of the star and her cat was named Bing in his honour. The oldest resident to live here was Annie Osborne who celebrated her 102nd birthday in July 1970. Longevity ran in the Osborne family for her brother celebrated his 100th birthday earlier in the same year at his home in Stockport, Cheshire. Annie was born in North Lambeth in 1868 and worked at the Brixton Independent Mission as well as for other charitable institutions. She moved to Wyatt Park Road in 1964 to live with her niece, Marion Godfellow.

Four

Streatham Common, The Rookery and Norwood Grove

The Lower Pond, Streatham Common, *c.* 1912. The Domesday Survey of 1086 lists a number of separate manors, or estates, which together comprised the ancient parish of Streatham. Among these was the manor of South Streatham which covered the land between Streatham Common and the fields on the south bank of the River Graveney, which formed the parish boundary with Croydon. The waste, or common land, of this manor was Streatham Common on which the manorial tenants had the right to graze their livestock and gather fuel. Until the late nineteenth century, local inhabitants still exercised these rights and Streatham Common maintained the appearance of an open field, not unlike the untended parts of Mitcham Common today. In 1888 the Metropolitan Board of Works paid £5 to the Ecclesiastical Commissioners, who were the Lords of the Manor of South Streatham, for conveying the 66 acres of common land to them in order to preserve it for all time as a public open space.

Streatham Common, *c.* 1912. After the Metropolitan Board of Works took over the Common they gradually 'tamed' the area. Paths were regulated to help limit soil erosion and provide a firm surface for people to walk on and by the mowing of the open grassland the western slope soon took on the appearance of public parkland. Under the terms of their purchase the Board was obliged to continue to maintain an area which had been chained off for many years for use by local cricket clubs. The view above shows a cricket match in progress before the First World War. Formal cricket games continued to be played on the Common well into the 1970s. The view below shows part of the horse ride which was laid out around the perimeter of the common by the Board. Prior to this riders were free to roam at their will but this was considered undesirable once more people used the area for recreational purposes.

The Lower Pond, Streatham Common, *c.* 1919. The pond at the bottom of Streatham Common originally served as a watering place for livestock grazing nearby and was a popular spot for children to paddle in the summer or skate in the winter. Although it covered a relatively small area, the pond was very deep and a number of people have drowned here, either by accident or by a deliberate wish to end their own lives. Suicides apart, the ponds on the Common were not very healthy places as we can gather from a survey of the parish in 1854 which reported: 'We find that some of the inhabitants complain of the pond at the corner of Streatham Common near to Mr S. Wilson's. The pond is too foul to supply water for cattle, and is of no use to the neighbourhood, and when partly dry (as it frequently is) the malaria arising there from is very injurious.' The view below shows the pond in the late 1930s.

Streatham Common South, *c.* 1919. This road started life as a seventeenth-century trackway from the High Road to the mineral wells at the top of the Common. These were first discovered in 1659 but it was not until some years later that the site was developed into Streatham Spa. This became a popular local attraction in the eighteenth century at which time it was not uncommon for carriages to queue for a mile along the High Road as visitors flocked to the area to take the Streatham waters.

Streatham Common South, *c.* 1914. One of the improvements initiated by the Board of Works when they took over the management of the common was to plant trees around the edge to screen off the buildings from public view. This helped maintain the rural aspect of the common and provided seasonal character to the open space. The young saplings seen here have now grown in to large mature trees. Note the tower of Immanuel church at the bottom of the hill.

Streatham War Memorial *c.* 1925. This commemorates the 720 local inhabitants who died in the First World War. It was designed by Albert Toft and was unveiled on 14 October 1922. Behind the statue can be seen The Chimes, a large Victorian house that was used as a club and social centre for ex-servicemen. The building was seriously damaged by a V1 bomb that fell nearby on 5 July 1944 and was subsequently demolished.

Streatham Common North, c. 1925. This ancient lane was one of the main routes to the detached part of Streatham parish at Knight's Hill. It also provided an impressive carriage drive to Hill House, a large mansion that stood at the top of the Common. This was the home of James Coster, whose family lived here with nine servants to cater for their needs. In his will James stipulated that he should be buried 'without the least ostentation, and direct that no hearse or other carriage shall be used or occupied at my funeral but that my remains be carried to the church and place of interment by forty poor industrious people including servants of my own and that each of them shall be paid for such service the sum of one guinea'. He died in 1857 aged seventy-three and a local inhabitant of the day recalled the body being carried, just as it was, down the Common and along the High Road to St Leonard's church where it was placed in the family vault.

Entrance to Park Hill, Streatham Common North, *c.* 1914. These views show the entrance gates and lodge of Park Hill, at the top of Streatham Common North, which survives today as St Michael's Convent. The house was built in around 1830 for William Leaf, a banker and successful silk merchant. The lodge was constructed by Leaf in 1870 and features his family crest and motto *Folium non defluet* (The leaf does not fall), under which the date 1870 is bisected by the interwoven initials WL. The sugar magnate Henry Tate, of Tate and Lyle, moved here in 1885 and spent the last fourteen years of his life in the house. Henry was a great philanthropist and gave generously for the building of Streatham Library (see p. 24). He was also a keen collector of paintings and every year would open his gallery at Park Hill for local people to see. He built the Tate Gallery in London and donated many of his finest works of art to the Gallery.

The Rookery, *c.* 1914. These beautiful public gardens were laid out in the grounds of a large house called the Rookery which stood on top of the terrace seen above. The house was demolished after the property was acquired by the London County Council, who laid out the gardens and opened them to the public in 1913. A former resident of the Rookery was Sir Kingsmill Grove Key, the only son of Sir John Key who was twice Lord Mayor of London. Sir Kingsmill was a keen cricketer and captained Surrey County Cricket Club from 1894 to 1899. From the 1850s until their death he and his wife hosted a special New Year's Day dinner for the poor of South Streatham which was held at the Beehive Coffee Tavern on Streatham High Road. The Rookery marks the spot of Streatham's original mineral wells and the grounds of the house were originally developed as an attraction for the many people who came here to take the waters in the seventeenth and eighteenth centuries.

The Rookery Gardens in the 1920s. The view above shows the Wishing Well in the Rookery gardens. This was the site of one of three original wells at the Rookery from which were obtained the mineral waters for which Streatham became famous. A visitor to the wells in the 1750s reported two wells then in use, the third having been filled up for 'some time'. Both of the surviving wells had been 'arched over' to secure them from the rains. However, as many local people had complained that the water drawn from the capped wells 'smelled strongly like boiled eggs' the proprietor opened one of them up. It is assumed that this is the well which survives today as the Wishing Well. The view below shows the White Garden, *c*. 1914. This contained only flowers with white blooms and even the park benches here were painted white to enhance the theme. This part of the Rookery was much admired by Queen Mary who made a number of visits here.

The Rock and Water Garden, The Rookery, *c.* 1914. To the south east of the terrace, hidden behind tall shrubs, is the rock and water garden which forms a pleasant secluded enclave within the Rookery. This part of the grounds was the location of an Ice House in which ice was stored in winter months for use during the summer. The owner of the Rookery had the right to take ice from the ponds on Streatham Common for storage in the ice house.

Streatham Common Woods, *c.* 1933. To the eastern end of Streatham Common lies an area of dense woodland. This was originally an extensive area of scrub land covered in bracken and furze from where local inhabitants would gather fuel for their fires. Following the acquisition of the Common by the Metropolitan Board of Works in 1888 the land here was allowed to grow into a wooded area which provides a number of delightful walks and a haven for birds and wildlife.

The driveway to Norwood Grove *c.* 1930. From the top of Streatham Common South a dirt road leads past the Rookery Gardens to Norwood Grove. Known as The Avenue, this route formed the carriage driveway to the Grove. The pillars of the gates which once barred entrance to the grounds of Norwood Grove survive today, as does the small gate lodge which is a Grade II listed building. The Lodge was built in 1860 and above the door is the motto *Patria fidelis* ('Faithful to the Fatherland') with the crest of an arm holding a hammer and the entwined letters of three As and an M. These no doubt stand for Arthur Anderson, and his wife Margaret, who moved to the Grove in 1847. Arthur Anderson was the joint founded the Peninsular & Oriental Steam Navigation Company, known today simply as the P&O line. From the driveway the Lodge appears to be a single-storey building but is in fact two storeys high with the front entrance on the upper floor.

Norwood Grove, *c.* 1930. The house was built in the early nineteenth century, since when it has been known under a number of different names, including Streatham Grove and the White House. In 1864 the famous Italian patriot, Garibaldi, dined with Arthur Anderson at Norwood Grove following which he visited the Crystal Palace. From 1878 to 1913 the house was occupied by Frederick Nettlefold and his family. In 1833 Frederick entered his father's iron and screw business and built the company up to become the first major manufacturer of pointed wood screws produced on automatic machinery in the world. The company survives today as part of the GKN Group, formerly known as Guest, Keen and Nettlefold. In 1924 a local resident, Stenton Covington, launched a successful campaign to acquire the Grove and its grounds for use as a public open space and they were opened by the Prince of Wales in November 1926.

The Sphinx stairway, Norwood Grove, *c.* 1930. A pair of large stone sphinxes used to guard the steps leading up to the orangery which runs along the eastern end of the house. These giant creatures proved to be a favourite attraction for children who would ride the beasts and have their photographs taken here. Sadly they have both now disappeared. However, the orangery remains to provide a sheltered area from which to enjoy the view over the surrounding countryside.

The parish boundary, Streatham Common/Norwood Grove, c. 1930. Running along the northern side of the railings which separate Streatham Common and Norwood Grove is a small ditch guarded by a stand of magnificent old oak trees. This line marks the ancient boundary between Streatham and Croydon parishes and a number of old parish boundary posts can still be seen among the trees. In wet weather a small stream still trickles along the ditch and disappears into a drain by the entrance to this part of the Common.